The
Story of Moses

By REV. JUDE WINKLER, OFM Conv.

S0-DOO-188

Imprimi Potest: Daniel Pietrzak, OFM Conv., Minister Provincial of St. Anthony of Padua Province (USA)
Nihil Obstat: Daniel V. Flynn, J.C.D., Censor Librorum
Imprimatur: Patrick J. Sheridan, Vicar General, Archdiocese of New York

The Hebrews are enslaved

MANY years had passed since Jacob and Joseph had brought their family down to Egypt. God had blessed the Hebrew people, and they had grown to become a great nation.

The Pharaoh of Egypt (the kings of Egypt were called Pharaohs) hated the Hebrews. He feared that if Egypt were to go to war, the Hebrews would side with their enemies.

So Pharaoh ordered that the Hebrews be made slaves and be forced to make bricks to build cities.

Moses is born

THE Hebrews grew stronger and Pharaoh became angry. He ordered that all the baby boys born to the Hebrews be thrown into the Nile.

A family from the tribe of Levi had a baby boy and they hid him until he was three months old. Then, because they could hide him no longer, they put him in a basket and laid it in the reeds that grew on the banks of the Nile.

The daughter of Pharaoh came to the river. She saw the basket and had it brought to her. When she opened it, she saw the baby.

Moses is taken to the palace

PHARAOH'S daughter knew this was a Hebrew baby but decided to adopt him. She called him "Moses"—"drawn from the water."

Moses' sister had been standing nearby to see what happened. She offered to find a nurse for the baby. She called her mother, and Pharaoh's daughter told her to care for the baby.

When Moses had grown, his mother brought him to the palace where he was treated like a prince of Egypt. Moses stayed there until he was forty years old.

Moses flees to the desert

ONE day, Moses saw an Egyptian strike a Hebrew slave. He became angry and struck the Egyptian, killing him.

Moses soon realized that Pharaoh was planning to have him put to death. And so Moses fled for his life, going into the desert of Midian.

Moses meets his wife

MOSES, tired from his journey, sat down near a well. He watched as the seven daughters of a priest of Midian, Jethro, brought their flocks to the well. The shepherds there treated them badly and drove their flocks away.

Moses went over to aid the young women. He drove the evil shepherds away and helped the women to water their flocks.

The daughters invited Moses to eat supper with them and their father. Jethro asked Moses to stay on with him, and Moses agreed. He eventually married Zipporah, one of Jethro's daughters, and they had two sons.

The burning bush

MOSES tended the flocks of Jethro, his father-in-law.

One day, he was out with the flock near Mount Horeb (which is also called Mount Sinai) when he saw a strange sight. He saw a bush that was on fire but was not burning up.

Moses decided to go up to see what was happening. As he approached the bush, he heard a voice that called out, "Moses! Moses!" Moses did not know what to make of this, but he answered, "Here I am."

7

God speaks to Moses

THE voice from the bush told Moses to take off his sandals for he was standing on holy ground. He then said He was the God of Abraham, the God of Isaac, and the God of Jacob.

He had heard the cries of His people in Egypt. He would now lead them from the land of their slavery to a land flowing with milk and honey. Moses was to go tell this to Pharaoh.

Moses asked the Lord what His name was so that he could tell the Hebrews. He answered that His name was "Yahweh," which means, "I am." He also taught Moses how to perform certain great signs to show that God had sent him.

Moses returns to Egypt

MOSES left his father-in-law and went back toward Egypt. He met Aaron, his brother, whom the Lord had sent out to meet him, for Aaron was to be a spokesman for Moses.

When they arrived in Egypt, they went before Pharaoh and told him that the God of Israel had a message for him. He was to let the Hebrews go into the desert where they would worship their God. Pharaoh refused to listen to them. Instead he became so angry that he ordered the Hebrew slaves to do more work.

God sends plagues against Egypt

GOD told Moses to go to the Nile and strike the water with his rod. When Moses did this, all the water in the river changed into blood. Pharaoh called his magicians who were able to perform the same deed. So Pharaoh would not allow God's people to leave.

Seven days after this, God sent Moses back to Pharaoh. Moses told Pharaoh that he must let the Hebrews go to serve the Lord or else God would send a plague of frogs all over the land.

But Pharaoh would not listen to Moses. Moses had Aaron stretch his hand out over the rivers and frogs covered the entire land. Pharaoh's magicians were again able to do the same thing. So Pharaoh refused to believe in the power of Moses and would not let his people go.

God sent more plagues against the land. The desert dust was changed into gnats, then there was a plague of flies. A disease broke out that killed the cattle, and both men and beasts were covered with boils. There was hail and lightning, locusts and even darkness that covered the whole land. But Pharaoh refused to budge.

One plague remained, one so horrible that Pharaoh would be forced to relent: the firstborn of every family in Egypt would die.

The Passover

MOSES ordered the Hebrews to prepare for that night when the Lord would free His people. They were to roast a lamb and eat it with unleavened bread and with bitter herbs. They were told to eat standing as if they were ready to leave for a journey, for they would soon be leaving the land of their slavery.

Each family was to mark its doorposts with some of the blood of the lamb. During that night the angel of death passed over the land. He killed all the firstborn in the entire land, both of man and of beast, but he passed over the houses where the doorposts were marked with blood.

The Hebrews leave Egypt

WHEN Pharaoh saw what had happened, he was greatly afraid. Even his own son had died in this plague. He called for Moses and Aaron in the middle of the night and he told them to take the Hebrews out of his land.

The Hebrews had not gone very far, though, when Pharaoh changed his mind. He gathered his army and chased after the Hebrews.

The Crossing of the Red Sea

THE Hebrews looked back and saw the Pharaoh's army chasing them and they looked ahead and saw the Red Sea. They were trapped and they felt they would surely die so they called out to the Lord.

God had Moses stretch out his hands over the Red Sea. As soon as he lifted up his arms, the Lord caused the great east wind to come up and it divided the waters of the sea. The Hebrews then passed on dry land through the Red Sea.

Pharaoh's army drowns in the Red Sea

PHARAOH saw what had happened, and he ordered his army to follow the Hebrews. However, his chariots were so heavy that the wheels began to get stuck in the mud, and they could not catch up with the Hebrews.

When all of the Hebrews had crossed the sea, God told Moses to stretch out his hands over the water one more time. He did this, and all of the waters that had been parted came crashing down upon the Egyptians. Not a single Egyptian escaped this terrible flood while not a single Hebrew had lost his life.

Moses and Miriam praise the Lord

THE Hebrews saw what great wonders God had worked for them and they celebrated because God had freed them from the land of their slavery.

Moses and the people sang to celebrate God's great love for them.

Then Miriam, the sister of Moses and Aaron, sang and danced with all of the women in the camp to thank the Lord for all the good things that He had done for them.

"The Lord gives me strength and courage,
and He is my Savior.

He is my God,
and I will praise Him.

Sing to the Lord,
for He is worthy of great honor.

He has hurled both horses and chariots
into the sea."

Food from heaven

THE people soon began to worry and complain for they did not have enough food. Had God brought them out to the desert to die?

The Lord answered them by telling Moses that He would cause bread to rain from the heavens. Each evening He would cause manna, a substance that looks like a small seed, to fall upon the ground. The Hebrews were to collect it each morning and to grind it for their bread.

The people were not even satisfied with this, for they complained that they did not have any meat. God sent flocks of quail to pass over their camp so that they could catch and cook them.

Water from a rock

EVEN then the people still did not trust God. They complained that they did not have any water and that they would surely die of thirst.

God told Moses to take his rod and strike a rock and water would flow out of it. Moses was greatly bothered by his people's complaints, and his faith began to waver. He struck the rock twice instead of once as the Lord had ordered him to do.

God caused water to spring forth from the rock, but he also punished Moses for his lack of faith. He told Moses that he would never enter into the Promised Land.

God protects the Hebrews
from their enemies

AS the Hebrew people crossed the desert, they came across some tribes that hated them—like the people of Amalek.

God told Moses to climb to the top of a hill that overlooked the field where the Hebrews and the men of Amalek would fight. Moses lifted up his arms in prayer, and as long as his arms were lifted, the Hebrews would win.

Aaron and Hur had gone up the hill with Moses and they held up his arms for Moses was too tired to hold them up alone. The Hebrews won a great victory that day over their enemies.

Moses climbs Mount Sinai

THE Hebrew people continued to wander in the desert until they came to the mountain where God had first spoken to Moses.

Moses ordered the people to prepare themselves to meet the Lord. They all washed and prayed and waited for the Lord.

On the third day, there was thunder and lightning and smoke on the mountain. Moses led the people out of the camp to the foot of the mountain. He then climbed the mountain and spoke with the Lord.

The Ten Commandments

WHILE Moses was on top of the mountain, the Lord gave him a set of laws, the Ten Commandments, which his people were to follow all of their days. They are:

1) I am the Lord your God. You shall not have strange gods before me.

2) You shall not take the name of the Lord, your God, in vain.

3) Remember to keep holy the Sabbath.

4) Honor your father and your mother.

5) You shall not kill.

6) You shall not commit adultery.

7) You shall not steal.

8) You shall not bear false witness against your neighbor.

9. You shall not covet your neighbor's wife.

10. You shall not covet your neighbor's goods.

These Ten Commandments were a special gift from God so that His people would know how to do what is good and to avoid those things that are evil.

God gave Moses two tablets upon which He had written these Ten Commandments.

The Golden Calf

IT did not take the Hebrews long to choose the evil way. They waited for Moses to come down from the mountain, but he stayed on top talking to God for a long time. After a while they began to think that he might not come back.

The Hebrews decided that they would have to take care of themselves. They went to Aaron and told him to make some idols for them. Aaron told them to gather all their gold rings and jewelry. He then melted the gold and formed a golden calf.

The people were pleased by their new god. They built an altar before it and offered it sacrifices. At last they had a god they could see.

The Lord then spoke to Moses and told him all the things that the Hebrews were doing. He was ready to destroy them, and He promised to make a new people with Moses as their father. Moses begged Him to have mercy on the Hebrews, and God decided to give them another chance.

Moses came down from the mountain and saw what the Hebrews were doing. He became so angry that he threw down the two tablets of the Ten Commandments, and they broke into pieces.

He then ordered that the golden calf be ground up until it was a fine dust. All of those who had worshiped the calf were forced to drink some of that dust mixed with water. He punished all those who had sinned and had the people pray for forgiveness.

When the people had prayed and asked God for forgiveness, God had Moses prepare two new tablets and bring them to the top of the mountain. To show that He forgave His people, God wrote His commandments on these tablets and had Moses bring them back to the people.

The tent of meeting

THE Lord told Moses that he should build a tent where the people could worship the Lord. The people were to bring all of their treasures, their gold and silver, their fine cloth and skins, their precious wood and stones, and give them all to Moses for use in this tent.

Moses had the people work for many days on this tent. They made an altar from wood, which they covered with gold. They sewed together all the cloth for the outer wall of the shrine and for the inner part of the shrine.

They also made all of the clothes for Aaron and his sons for they would be their priests.

These priests were to offer sacrifices to the Lord to thank God for all the good things that He had done for His people and to ask for His pardon for any sins that they might have committed against Him.

The holiest part of the shrine was called the Holy of Holies. No one was allowed into the Holy of Holies except the high priest. It was there that Moses ordered the Ark of the Covenant to be kept.

The Ark of the Covenant

THE Ark of the Covenant was a wooden box covered with pure gold. It had two poles attached to its sides so that it could be carried in procession. On top of the Ark were two angels whose wings met in the middle. It was here that God would show Himself whenever He appeared to His people.

Some of the Hebrew's most holy objects were kept in the Ark. Moses ordered that the two tablets of the Ten Commandments, a bit of the manna, and Aaron's rod be placed inside of it.

The Bronze Serpent

IN spite of all these signs of God's love, the people still complained and sinned against Him. God once again had to punish His people. He sent poisonous snakes into the camp and they bit many of the Hebrews.

Moses begged the Lord to have mercy on His people. The Lord had Moses make a bronze serpent, and he put it on a pole. All of those who looked upon the bronze serpent with faith were cured. This bronze serpent was a type of promise, for many years later Jesus would be hung on a cross and all who looked upon Him with faith would be healed of their sins.

Moses makes Joshua his successor

WHEN Moses was old and dying, he chose Joshua to be the next leader of the people. Joshua had been one of the twelve spies who had entered the Promised Land. Only he and Caleb reported that they could defeat the people of that land if only they trusted in the Lord.

Moses sees the Promised Land and dies

MOSES led his people until he was one hundred and twenty years old. The Lord had decreed that Moses would never set foot in the Promised Land, but the Lord did let him see the land that was flowing with milk and honey.

God had Moses climb up Mount Nebo, which overlooked the Promised Land. He showed Moses this special land from north to south, east to west. Then Moses died and went home to God.

The people mourned thirty days, for Moses had been a great prophet and friend of God.

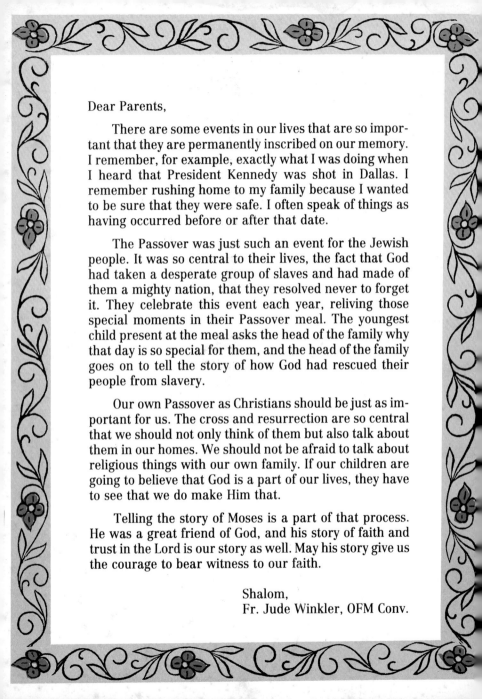

Dear Parents,

There are some events in our lives that are so important that they are permanently inscribed on our memory. I remember, for example, exactly what I was doing when I heard that President Kennedy was shot in Dallas. I remember rushing home to my family because I wanted to be sure that they were safe. I often speak of things as having occurred before or after that date.

The Passover was just such an event for the Jewish people. It was so central to their lives, the fact that God had taken a desperate group of slaves and had made of them a mighty nation, that they resolved never to forget it. They celebrate this event each year, reliving those special moments in their Passover meal. The youngest child present at the meal asks the head of the family why that day is so special for them, and the head of the family goes on to tell the story of how God had rescued their people from slavery.

Our own Passover as Christians should be just as important for us. The cross and resurrection are so central that we should not only think of them but also talk about them in our homes. We should not be afraid to talk about religious things with our own family. If our children are going to believe that God is a part of our lives, they have to see that we do make Him that.

Telling the story of Moses is a part of that process. He was a great friend of God, and his story of faith and trust in the Lord is our story as well. May his story give us the courage to bear witness to our faith.

Shalom,
Fr. Jude Winkler, OFM Conv.